AF496472

HERTFORDSHIRE

The Glorious County

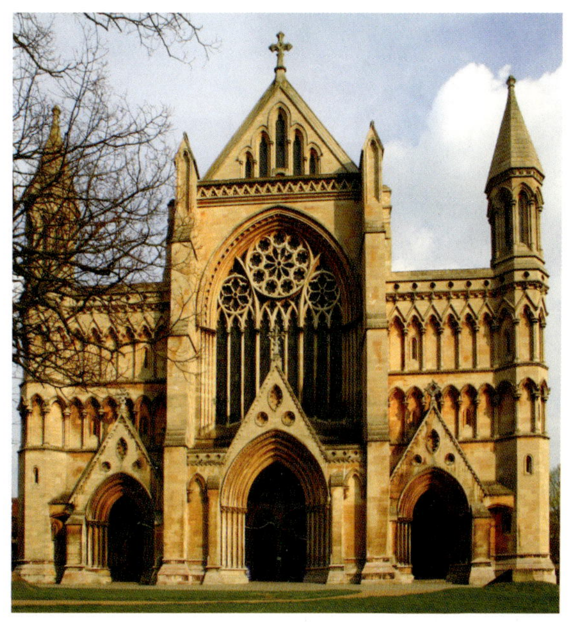

JUNE AND MICHAEL MASSEY

First published in Great Britain in 2008

British Library Cataloguing-in-Publication Data
A CIP record for this title is available from the British Library

ISBN 978 1 84114 716 1

HALSGROVE
Halsgrove House
Ryelands Industrial Estate
Bagley Road, Wellington, Somerset TA21 9PZ
Tel: 01823 653777   Fax: 01823 216796
email: sales@halsgrove.com
website: www.halsgrove.com

Printed and bound by
Grafiche Flaminia, Italy

INTRODUCTION

In this book we have tried to present a personal selection of images which we believe demonstrate some of the myriad glories of Hertfordshire. In addition to well-known and much-loved features, we have added some of the more unusual and hidden treasures to be found in the four corners of the county.

The complex history of Hertfordshire is reflected in the many different features – geographical, topographical, natural, artificial, sociological and architectural – that make up its landscape and its people. In geological times much of the county was covered by a lagoonal arm of the North Sea, giving rise to smooth contours and, amongst other geological features, the renowned Hertfordshire Puddingstone.

In more recent periods the Romans found this area a hotbed of resistance and rebellion, but still succeeded in establishing thriving cities such as St Albans and many wealthy villas, such as the one at Lockleys in Welwyn. Three of their major roads, Watling Street (A5), Akeman Street (A41) and Ermine Street (old A10), still run through the county.

The landed aristocracy have always found Hertfordshire, which enjoys close proximity to London, a congenial and convenient location to establish their huge estates – at Old Hatfield, Capel Manor, Knebworth, to name just three. Elizabeth the First became Queen of England in Hertfordshire, and Queen Elizabeth, the Queen Mother, was born here. Jane Austen and Charles Dickens both found settings for their novels here, and other literary links include George Orwell (Wallington, near Baldock), Charles Lamb (Westmill, near Buntingford), E M Forster (Old Stevenage), Graham Greene (Berkhampstead), Francis Bacon (St Albans), George Bernard Shaw (Ayot St Lawrence) and H G Wells (Hay Street, near Braughing).

Many substantial coaching towns, such as Hitchin, Baldock, Barnet and Hatfield, ensured that Hertfordshire was a vital link in the developing travel network of the eighteenth and early nineteenth centuries, while the rivers, growing web of canals, then railways and finally trunk roads have had a marked influence on the shape and character of the county.

Hertfordshire has played host to the two original 'Garden Cities' – Letchworth and Welwyn Garden City – founded in a genuine spirit of social regeneration by the visionary Ebenezer Howard in the early years of the twentieth century, and thus enjoyed the benefits of revolutionary styles of urban architecture and social experimentation. The Henry Moore Foundation at Perry Green reminds us that contemporary art, too, has found a home in the county.

Hertfordshire has an interesting and unusual industrial history, welcoming activities as diverse as film-making, brewing, aeronautical engineering and cereal production! Alfred Hitchcock made films at the Welwyn Studios, Stanley Kubrick chose to live near St Albans, and major Hollywood studios still use the resources of the Elstree-Borehamwood complex to make their contemporary blockbusters. The Hertford brewing firm of McMullen carries on a county-wide tradition, as do tiny independent breweries, such as the one at Green Tye. The aeronautical industry, centred on Hatfield, put down some very firm roots here, and it is an intriguing coincidence that the world's first balloonist, Vincenzo Lunardi, took to the air from London in 1784 and landed in Hertfordshire twice, once at Welham Green, and finally came to earth near Dane End. The industry is now commemorated at the De Havilland Aircraft Heritage Centre at Salisbury Hall, near London Colney, where many historic aircraft are preserved, including the prototype of the famous Mosquito. Shredded Wheat, originally known as 'Welgar Shredded Wheat' was still made until recently in the imposing art-deco factory in Welwyn Garden City.

Amid such diversity Hertfordshire still manages to provide huge swathes of countryside, farming land and horse-riding country, as well as hundreds of acres of open parkland and woodland for the leisure enjoyment of its varied population. This diversity is also reflected in the many different styles of dwellings throughout the county, including clapboard, redbrick, thatched and half-timbered construction, and the varied patterns of pargeting and whitewashed façades. We have tried to provide a selection of these in our collection.

Although our grounding in the visual image has been an analogue one, we are now more than happy to embrace the digital age. We have tried to combine dramatic images with those that reflect the life of Hertfordshire, town and country, and we hope that you will find both unusual perspectives on familiar places and ideas for new experiences.

We are aware that some of you will spot what you may regard as glaring omissions – every collection of this kind is bound to be selective – but we have also had to work within the constraints of copyright issues, which means that some familiar Hertfordshire landmarks are not permitted to be featured here. By contrast, we should like to acknowledge the cooperation of the many organisations and owners of properties who have kindly allowed us to represent them pictorially, including Knebworth House (www.knebworthhouse.com), The Henry Moore Foundation at Perry Green, The Welwyn Roman Baths, Mill Green Museum, The De Havilland Aircraft Heritage Centre, Rye Meads Nature Reserve, Hertfordshire Holly, Hopleys Nurseries, The Eight Bells public house in Hatfield, The Green Tye Brewery, St Albans Organ Theatre and Museum, The Rivers Orchard, Dr Edward Eastwood of the Clinton-Baker Pinetum at Bayfordbury, Simon Dennis Butchers of Sawbridgeworth and Mr and Mrs Ribbons (present owners of Braughing Station), and to thank them for sharing their knowledge and expertise so generously.

Although, between us, we have spent a total of some seventy years in Hertfordshire, we have certainly discovered many new facets of the county. We should like to thank the many friendly and helpful Hertfordshire folk we have met on our travels. We should also like to thank Chris and Betty Wedlake for their encouragement and enthusiasm for our work. Finally our gratitude goes to our friends and family for their helpful comments and often well-placed criticism.

Hertfordshire does not possess a majestic coastline, imposing mountains or rugged geology, but its glories past and present are multifarious nonetheless – rustic, urban, water-bound and land-locked, open-spaced and close-packed – and our personal choice of images attempts to reflect this variety: across the day, across the year, across the county.

Above: On a frosty winter morning the Stort mirrors this peaceful riverside scene.

Left: The dramatic vapour trails of passing aircraft slice through the dawn sky
and make a stunning reflection in the River Stort.

The 56-metre high Victorian spire of the Norman church of St Michael's in Bishops Stortford is a well-known local landmark which dominates the town from its lofty position on Windhill.

It's nice to know that you can still find some attractive village streets,
such as this one in Sawbridgeworth, totally devoid of cars!

Hertfordshire has always thrived on waterways, although boating on the Stort is now mainly for leisure.

Tissiman's of Bishops Stortford is believed to be the oldest company in the UK, the original buildings dating from 1360, with 'modernisations' in 1530!

Above: Reflected in the modern windows of the council offices are reminders of Hertfordshire's brewing tradition – the converted maltings in Bishops Stortford town centre. In the background is St Michael's church.

Right: The afternoon sun brings peace and tranquillity to this autumnal scene in Birchanger Woods.

Above: A common sight alongside Hertfordshire roads is fields of rape stretching into the distance.

Left: The golden evening sun bathes the old Sawbridgeworth maltings standing beside the
River Stort, once a crucial part of Hertfordshire's brewing industry.

The proud sign of the Green Tye Brewery (located behind the Prince of Wales pub, one of many such small independent breweries), some samples of the brew, and a statue of a maltmaker in Ware are all tasteful reminders of one of Hertfordshire's foremost industries.

Above: Henry Moore's figure at Perry Green appears to take on the persona of a guardian shepherd.

Left: This massive sculpture by Henry Moore – The Arch – stands out against its natural setting with striking form and colour.

Above: A tapestry of late-summer colours delights the eye in the garden of Hopley's Nursery.

Left: A striking and dramatic sculpture, part of the unique Henry Moore collection at Perry Green.

The gardens of Hopley's Nursery in Much Hadham offer a relaxing
and inspirational vista for the enthusiastic gardener.

St Andrew's, Much Hadham, a typical village church scene, complete with grazing sheep!

Fields lying under a heavy winter frost near Puckeridge.

The classic half-timbering of a cottage in Much Hadham.

A striking view of the majestic Digswell viaduct which has carried the
East Coast main line over the Mimram Valley since the mid-1850s.

The refurbished signal box, complete with fire bucket, at preserved Braughing station, now a private residence, provides a gentle reminder of the more leisurely era of branch-line steam travel from St Margarets to Buntingford.

A Nigel Gresley A4 Pacific locomotive thunders across the viaduct in appropriate 1950s monochrome.

The majestic sails of Cromer Post Mill, the only
surviving post mill in Hertfordshire.

Sunshine and shadow stride across the land near The Pelhams.

A fine stone bridge, spanning the River Lea, once carried
a major road through the quiet village of Stanstead Abbots.

In the absence of a coastline Hertfordshire residents can enjoy the delights of stunning
river views such as this breezy moment on the Lea at Stanstead Abbots.

Above: A reminder that Hertfordshire's aeronautical industry has natural roots! The Rye Meads Nature Reserve attracts a host of diverse wild life, such as this dragonfly.

Left: Neither new, nor a river, the New River, a man-made aqueduct, here seen at St Margarets, has been supplying water from springs at Ware to North London for over four hundred years!

Above: The classic picturesque village of Benington.

Left: This solitary swan enjoys the tranquil seclusion of a lake at Rye Meads Nature Reserve.

Left, inset: No solitude for the bevy of town-dwellers lining up for a 'swan quadrille' on the river at Ware!

The stunning façade of Knebworth House. The house originally dated from the early 1600s, but underwent major reconstruction in the nineteenth century.

One of Edwin Lutyens' most remarkable churches, St Martin's church,
Knebworth, was only completed in the 1960s.

Above: Herds of deer have roamed the estate of Knebworth Park since the fourteenth century.

Right: Bracken and fern carpet the forest floor of Bramfield.

The swirling skirts and dazzling footwork of 'Hertfordshire Holly' bring the clog morris dancing tradition to a local village pub.

The fishermen of Stanborough Lakes remind us that Isaak Walton, The Compleat Angler, enjoyed fishing in Hertfordshire.

A dramatic view of the 'business end' of the Welwyn Roman bath house, excavated as part of a villa complex and now entombed below the A1(M) near Welwyn in its own small museum. In the absence of any surviving Ancient Romans, it now comes complete with plaster cast slave to do the stoking!

The stately art deco lines of Welwyn Garden City's famous Shredded Wheat Factory are
a perfect example of the interrelationship between form and function.

The bold lines of this award-winning design make the swimming centre in
Hatfield a unique example of modern architecture.

A detail of the complex machinery installed in the impressively rebuilt flour mill at
Mill Green, near Hatfield, where a mill has stood for a thousand years.

Mill Green still produces flour for local bakers and houses a delightful local history museum.

The bustle of a typical Hertfordshire market, this one held in St Albans, reminds us that the county is as much about its people as it is its landscape.

45

A short section of Roman red tile and flint wall, close to the line of the original Watling Street, marks the boundary of Verulamium, the modern St Albans.

A large and stately church graces the village of Lemsford, with a single parishioner enjoying the lunchtime sun.

Above: This impressive Victorian addition to the Abbey church in St Albans marks the end of building development that spans some 1600 years.

Left: The lakes and lush autumnal colours of the parkland of Verulam Park make a perfect setting for this view of St Albans Abbey.

The Old Fighting Cocks in St Albans is said to be the oldest pub in England.

The superb and original art deco styling
of Letchworth's Broadway cinema.

The essence of Hertfordshire's agricultural scene – tracks,
crops and seemingly endless fields near Buntingford.

Right: A closer view of the green velvet fields near Cottered
as they unfold across the landscape.

One of the ideals of the garden city movement encapsulated in this study of
the historic Spirella factory (now a listed building) in Letchworth.

Ordered urban spaces, such as The Broadway in Letchworth, are one of the hallmarks of the garden city ideal.

Ancient Egypt comes to Baldock! This frieze now decorates the local Tesco, once the Kayser Bondor hosiery factory, but originally a film studio!

This archetypal scene, complete with ducks, is a major feature of the tiny village of Chapmore End,
near Bengeo, where The Woodman pub still serves beer directly from the barrel, keeping the
Hertfordshire tradition of brewing and selling beer very much alive.

The Woodman pub, Chapmore End.

These narrowboats at Broxbourne are a reminder of the former importance of
canals and rivers for the commerce of the county.

Left: The ever-important water supply at Dobb's Weir, near Broxbourne.

Detail of the carving from
the Eleanor Cross.

One of the only three remaining 'Eleanor Crosses', this one
at Waltham Cross, erected by Edward the First, marking
the resting place of Queen Eleanor's funeral procession on
its way from Lincoln to London in 1290.

A truly elegant setting for this dawn scene on Hadley Common.

Passing aircraft from Stansted make dramatic patterns in the evening sky over Green Tye.

The richness of a clear winter sky is captured in one of the two duck-ponds on Hadley Green.

This majestic archway, now known as Gobions Folly, once stood at the entrance to a magnificent country park near Potters Bar and is now all that remains of the estate.

The late afternoon sun and a sudden
shower combine to produce one of the
true wonders of nature, here seen
over the low Hertfordshire
landscape near Hunsdon.

The stark silhouette of trees at twilight dominates the uplands of Pishiobury Park on the Hertfordshire/Essex border.

A lone tree stands sentinel over a winter field straddling the border between Hertfordshire and Essex.

St Andrew's church, Little Berkhampstead, with its unusual wooden tower, is glimpsed through the lych gate.

A modern interpretation of the hart, the
symbol of Hertfordshire, provides a striking
frontispiece for County Hall, Hertford. The
site of the General Synod of 673 AD
which determined the rules for the calculation
of Easter is believed to be in Hertford.

The hart in close-up.

Hertford Castle seems to act as an imposing gateway to the town.

The striking geometric lines of the clock tower in Stevenage town centre underline the modernity of new-town design.

Bowling Green and the war memorial, Old Stevenage.

At one time railways criss-crossed Hertfordshire, but many branch lines are now remembered only as picturesque country walks, such as the Ayot Greenway between Hatfield and Dunstable.

This tranquil view at Ayot St Peter could be a scene from a Jane Austen novel.

The neo-Palladian church in Ayot St Lawrence which replaced the disused building featured in the photograph on page 76.

A detail of the stunning ceiling decoration in this neo-classical church.

The derelict tower of the former church at Ayot St Lawrence stands out against a summer sky.

A view of the defensive ditch, known locally as the Devil's Dyke, dug by the ancient Britons to defend their stronghold against the might of Julius Caesar's army.

THIS ENTRENCHMENT
IS PART OF A
BRITISH CITY
BUILT IN THE
1ST CENTURY B.C.
IT WAS PROBABLY HERE THAT
JULIUS CAESAR
DEFEATED THE BRITISH KING
CASSIVELLAUNUS
IN 54 B C

Above: The magnificent expanse of Harpenden Common once had its own racecourse.

Left: Devil's Dyke sign– as the sign indicates, the Romans' long and
settled connection with Hertfordshire began here near Wheathampstead.

Rothampstead, an attractive country estate, now the site of a scientific research centre, still plays
host to botanical experiments which began over one hundred and fifty years ago!

Redbournbury, one of the few surviving working mills in Hertfordshire.

A unique feature of Hertfordshire's cultural scene – St Albans Organ Theatre and Museum, founded by Charles Hart, housing this magnificent Mortier 97-key Belgian dance hall organ and many other mechanical musical instruments and memorabilia. We enjoyed one of the regular Sunday afternoon concerts and free tea!

Salisbury Hall, near London Colney, is the place where Sir Nigel Gresley designed his A4 Pacific steam locomotive, and Sir Geoffrey De Havilland designed and built the prototype of the De Havilland Mosquito.

The building next to Salisbury Hall was where Nell Gwynn 'entertained' Charles II.

The spring blossom on these apple trees, all that remains of the world-famous Thomas Rivers Orchard, near Sawbridgeworth, where the conference pear was first developed. The orchard is now maintained by a dedicated group of volunteers.

A De Havilland Mosquito, a powerful reminder of Hertfordshire's aeronautical glories.
This and the one opposite are both are to be seen at the De Havilland Heritage Centre.

The priceless prototype of the De Havilland Mosquito.

The richness of ripe apples brings a depth of colour to a Hertfordshire garden near the orchard.

The village of Standon, bathed in the brightness of the afternoon sun, is seen nestling in the valley.

A quiet corner in the village of Standon.

An example of the unique geology of the county – Hertfordshire Puddingstone.

Above: This magnificent old school house in Standon makes an impressive image.

Right: The early birds obviously on worm-catching duties near Puckeridge.

A view across the countryside through the old lych gate at Anstey.

The attractive village hall in the village of Wallington, near Baldock. It was here that
George Orwell took up residence and ran the village store in the late 1930s.

These two views typify the green-field topography of East Hertfordshire.

Note the dolphins
on the pargetting of the
Ashwell Guildhouse.

The peace and quiet of Ashwell Springs.

Hertfordshire abounds in village greens. This lush example is in Cottered.

The village stocks at Brent Pelham, a reminder of the brutality of ancient justice.
We would like to think that the tree provided some welcome shade for the guilty miscreants!

A view of Brent Pelham across the surrounding fields.

The verdant fields near Brent Pelham.

A once-familiar sight in many
Hertfordshire and Essex villages, these
clapboard cottages in Hunsdon retain their
picture postcard appearance.

What could be more English
than afternoon tea at the
Westmill Tea Rooms?

The village green, Westmill, is often regarded as the quintessential Hertfordshire village.
The writer, Charles Lamb, lived here for some time.

This scene at Westmillbury captures the essence of rural peace and tranquillity in 'Charles Lamb' country.

The unusual 'one-handed' clock in Buntingford's High Street.

The North Hertfordshire town of Royston
can still boast cobbled sidestreets.

The elegant and ornate
thatching of cottages
in Barkway.

Ware Priory, dating
from the 1400s,
originally a friary and
now a function suite.

This Grade II listed building houses a local butcher who continues a tradition of over one hundred years of uninterrupted meat provision in the Market Square in Sawbridgeworth.

Local shops, this one bringing a breath of Gallic air, are often half-hidden treasures to be found in many a Hertfordshire village.

One of Hertfordshire's well-known rivers, the Lea, meanders past a unique group of eighteenth century gazebos in Ware. In the background stand the maltings buildings, another reminder of Hertfordshire's long brewing tradition.

The village duck-pond in Barkway.

The traditional house decoration known as pargetting is well-represented in many Hertfordshire villages.

Some of the magnificent pines preserved in the Clinton-Baker Pinetum at Bayfordbury,
deemed to be one of Hertfordshire's best kept secrets.

The country comes to town! A quieter moment in Aldenham Country Park, near Radlett, one of London's playgrounds.

The cows share the peace of Aldenham Country Park.

A tranquil scene by
the river in Watford's
Cassiobury Park, once
a great estate.

The town comes to the country! 1930s' Watford Station, the end of the tube,
set in the leafy suburbs of John Betjeman's metroland.

Croxley Green, the small town near Watford, once the home of John Dickinson's paper mills. The sign on the bench reads: 'Croxley Green Conservation Area. To conserve the rare wild flowers and grasses, this part of The Green is left in its natural state.'

Trees now dominate the derelict walls of a once-proud castle in Berkhamstead,
which has had some form of fortification since the eleventh century.

Baldock church is a
classic example of the
'Hertfordshire Spike' steeple.

Narrow boats on the
Stort are a continuing
reminder of the
importance of waterways
in the county.

A view from
Benington
Lordship across the
magnificent gardens.

Above: A sunny view of Benington Lordship, where visitors are enjoying a 'Snowdrop Sunday'.

Left: The humble snowdrop makes a stunning contribution to the beauty of Benington Lordship.

St Mary's church in the centre of Hitchin dates from the fifteenth century, and its substantial size is a mark of the wealth of the mediaeval wool trade centred on the town.

Hitchin Priory, originally a fourteenth-century Carmelite monastery, was rebuilt in the Georgian period as a private house, and now serves as a conference centre.

Above: A volunteer at the Clinton-Baker Pinetum at Bayfordbury nicknamed this specimen 'the ballerina tree', because of its ethereal beauty.

Left: A 'fairy grotto' amid the bracken and fern in Bramfield Forest.

A country road sweeps across the landscape near Dane End.

St Etheldreda's, the parish church of Hatfield, dating originally from the thirteenth century, although much reconstructed in later periods, is known locally as St Audrey's, which has given the word 'tawdry' to the English language as a mark of the dubious quality of goods available at the market in mediaeval times. According to Dickens *(Oliver Twist)*, this is the church passed by Bill Sikes on his way down the hill to the Eight Bells inn at the bottom of Fore Street.

The trees, green spaces and the red-brick architecture of the houses are the typical features of Ebenezer Howard's vision of the 'City in the Garden' that is Welwyn Garden City.

A Hertfordshire woodturner displays his range of exquisite wooden products for sale at Barnet's monthly craft fair.

The quintessential market scene at Barnet's historic open air market.

131

A golden sunset over Stanborough Lakes.

It is believed that Charles Dickens used the Eight Bells in Old Hatfield as the inspiration for the pub that Bill Sikes made his way to at nightfall after killing Nancy in *Oliver Twist*.

"It was nine o'clock at night, when the man, quite tired out, and the dog, limping and lame from the unaccustomed exercise, turned down the hill by the church of the quiet village, and plodding along the little street, crept into a small public house, whose scanty light had guided them to the spot. There was a fire in the tap-room and some country-labourers were drinking before it"

Charles Dickens – *Oliver Twist*

The rolling green parkland on the Herts/Essex border at Pishiobury Park.

Above: Kingsbury Water Mill, once the abbot's malt mill dating from the sixteenth century and now a museum and restaurant, basks in the spring sun.

Right: Pleasure boats stacked up at Broxbourne Lido, awaiting holiday mariners.

The old English pub, The Three Horseshoes, at Spellbrook, originally dating from the seventeenth century.

The church of St Peter and St Paul in Tring, mostly dates from the
fifteenth century, although a church has stood here since 1100.

Left: The Icknield Way, the oldest prehistoric road in Britain, stretches from Buckinghamshire to Norfolk, and here marks the county boundary between Hertfordshire and Bedfordshire.

A breathtaking view over the open countryside of the Herts/Beds border.

The historic Fair Green in Sawbridgeworth, protected from development by ancient statute which requires an annual fair to be held there.

Deacon Hill,
a high point
in the Chilterns.

The church of Our Lady
at Puttenham, with
its very picturesque
fifteenth-century
chequered flint and
stone tower.

Above: This stretch of the Grand Union Canal in the centre of Berkhamstead must have been a familiar sight to novelist Graham Greene, whose father was the headmaster of nearby Berkhamstead School.

Left: Another view of the rolling hills of the Chilterns, south of Tring.

The long day closes. Constantly changing colours bring another vivid panorama to the evening sky over Hertfordshire.